Memories of Co. Limerick's Railways
A. H. Vaughan

No. 303 was built to the designs of Robert Coey for the Great Southern & Western Railway in 1900. It had two inside cylinders 18 in. x 26 in. working on 6 ft 7 in. driving wheels served by steam at 160 lbs psi. Awaiting scrapping c.1959 at Limerick Engine Shed.

© A. H. Vaughan, 2022
First published in the United Kingdom, 2022,
by Stenlake Publishing Ltd.
www.stenlake.co.uk
ISBN 978-1-84033-957-4

The publishers regret that they cannot supply copies of any pictures featured in this book.

Printed by
Claro Print, Office 26, 27, 1 Spiersbridge Way,
Thornliebank, Glasgow G46 8NG

Introduction

Most of the photos were taken by me using my 1958 Rolleiflex Model 'T' between 1974 and 1982. But there are four by Peter Barlow using a medium format camera in 1956. It was a great pleasure to spend a day out in the sun, looking for railways signals and signal boxes to photograph.

Visits to the different places led to some happy conversations with the signalmen. In Limerick Check cabin, I had the good fortune to meet a young and sympathetic signalman, Tommy O'Brien. Tommy eventually became 'Signalmen's' Inspector'. At Dromkeen the signalman was very friendly. I said that I would love to do but had promised to be home for lunch. I hope these pictures of the old mechanical railway will give the reader as much pleasure as I got taking the photos.

Adrian Vaughan,
Barney. May 2023

Acknowledgements

Inside Ballingrane Junction Signal Box, peeping round the door post is a little girl, surely from the station house. I am indebted to her for enlivening the scene. I must thank for their kind assistance with captions: Reg Instone, Anthony Gray, Andrew Faulkner, Mick Deady, and Paul Dodson. The Signalling Record Society's Irish Signal Box Register was also helpful.

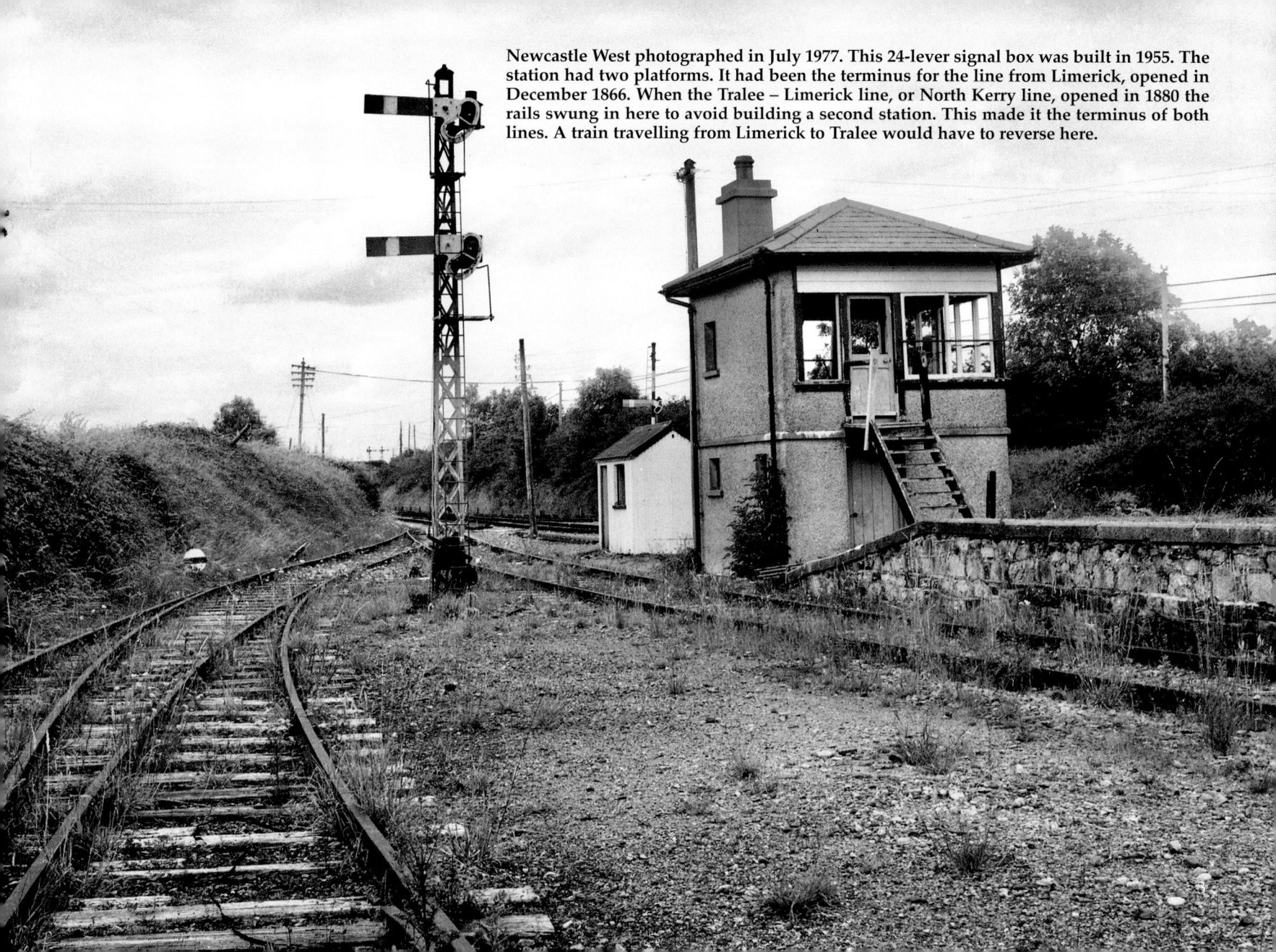

Newcastle West photographed in July 1977. This 24-lever signal box was built in 1955. The station had two platforms. It had been the terminus for the line from Limerick, opened in December 1866. When the Tralee – Limerick line, or North Kerry line, opened in 1880 the rails swung in here to avoid building a second station. This made it the terminus of both lines. A train travelling from Limerick to Tralee would have to reverse here.

Facing page: Newcastle West in July 1977, looking outwards from the signal box. A pair of crossovers allow either side of the platform to be used for Tralee- or Limerick-bound trains.

Newcastle West. Saxby & Farmer signal, *c.*1910, signals on the Limerick line routing to either platform, also a small signal below, main arms routing to a siding. The Tralee line is on the left. Closed in November 1975. July 1977

Rathkeale Signal Box interior, July 1977. The 17 lever signal box was in use from 1895 to November 1975.

Facing page: Looking towards Newcastle West from Rathkeale Station in July 1977, the Down Home signal, ground disc signal for the siding and signal box beyond.

Looking towards Limerick from Rathkeale, July 1977.

The station master's handsome house of 1858, at Ballingrane Junction, May 1982. Cut limestone right up to the chimney stacks. Next to it is the fine limestone goods shed with the station offices and platforms on the other side.

Looking through Ballingrane Junction Station from the Limerick end, May 1982.

Facing page: The signal box at Ballingrane Junction was built in 1895 but was rebuilt in 1923. The view, photographed in May 1982, is towards the Newcastle/ Foynes Junction. My wife, Susan, is admiring the box. The signal beyond the crossing gates marks the junction where the branch to Foynes began.

Inside the box were the Railway Signal Co. levers numbered to 28. The Webb-Thompson Large Electric Staff machine out of use in July 1974 was for the section to Rathkeale. The minature Electric Staffs for Foynes.

The junction with the Foynes Branch. The Saxby & Farmer (S&F) Up Foynes Branch Home signal. The North Kerry line is on the right, the crossing gates and signal box beyond.

The Up North Kerry line Home signal, Ballingrane Junction.

Ballingrane Junction. No. 184 just returned from Foynes. The train was then reversed to the North Kerry line for a nostalgic recreation of a long gone scene.

The branch that served Foynes Harbour on the Shannon closed to passenger trains in November 1965, but remained open for freight until 2000. The harbour was busy in January 1974.

Tons of freight arriving behind 004 at Foynes, January 1974. The facing page shows wagons at the quayside with a Soviet cargo ship alongside.

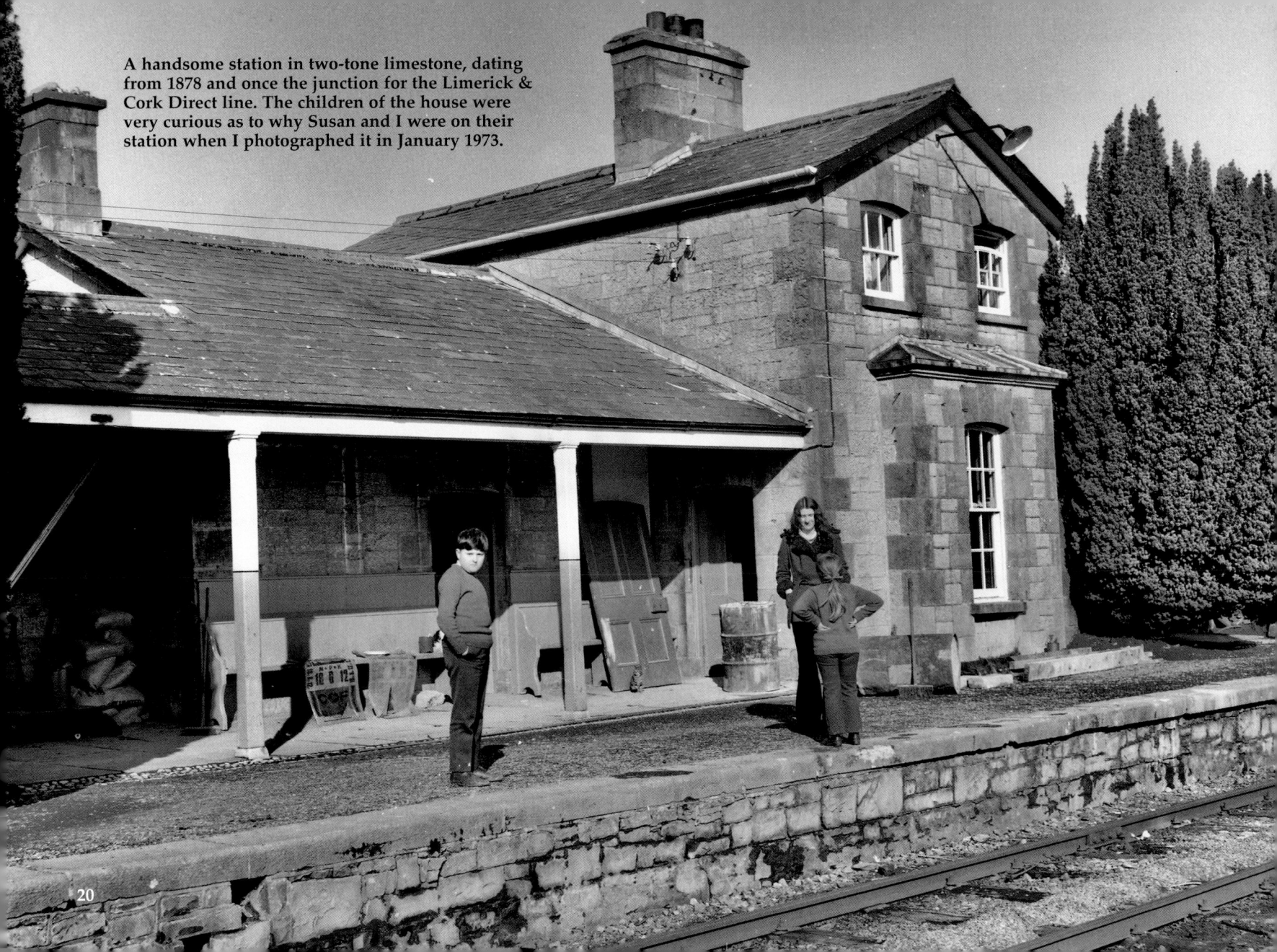

A handsome station in two-tone limestone, dating from 1878 and once the junction for the Limerick & Cork Direct line. The children of the house were very curious as to why Susan and I were on their station when I photographed it in January 1973.

The original signal box was destroyed in the Civil War and rebuilt with a 24-lever GS&WR lever frame in November 1923. The route to Cork was closed to passenger trains in 1934 and closed to goods in 1967.

Facing page: Patrickswell, looking towards Limerick. The signal box – open only 'as required' – was switched out with signals cleared.

A closer view of the antique box van and a Saxby & Farmer signal still handsome after standing there for maybe 65 years. The ground disc signalled into the siding. The bolt mechanism, which holds the points firm whichever way they lie, can just be seen between the rails.

Facing page: After Patrickswell comes Foynes Junction and Carey's Road sidings on the outskirts of Limerick. The points are set for Limerick Check Signal Box in this August 1956 photograph. The other setting way would lead to the terminus Colbert. The points were operated electrically from Limerick Check. On the right some rodding crosses to the left and operated the points to and from the single track. The points were worked by hand lever which was locked until released electrically from Limerick Check. *Peter Barlow*

The station signal box was built in 1892 with 20 levers, was extended to hold 78 levers in 1910 and rendered over in cement. The tip of the signal arm routing to the North Kerry line peeps in on the extreme left. The route to Newcastle West, left foreground, was closed to passenger traffic on 4th February 1963. In 1973 the mechanical signalling at the station was abolished for push button electric controls. *Peter Barlow*

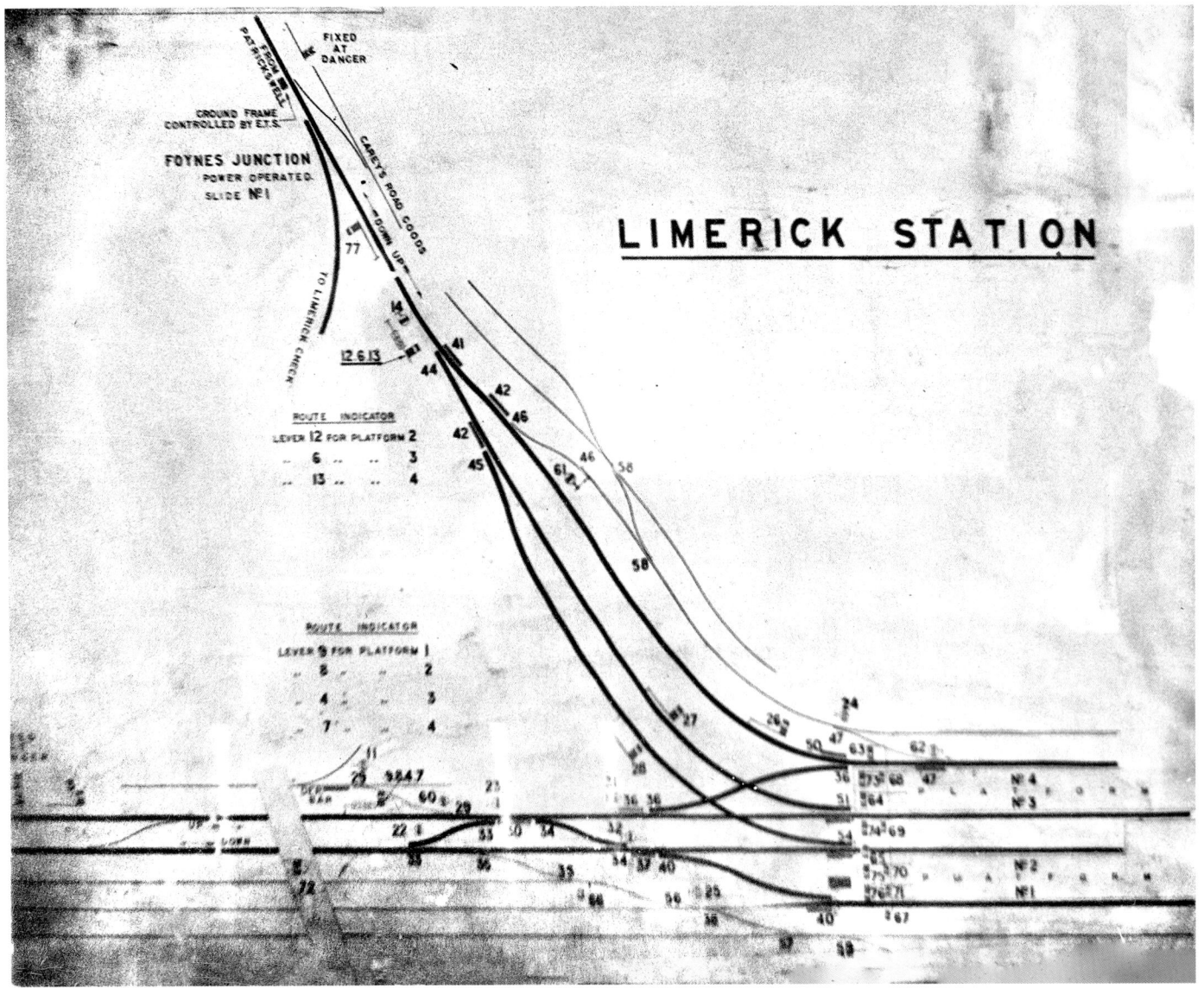

Limerick Colbert Signal Box track diagram, August 1956, showing platforms 2, 3 and 4 with connections to the North Kerry (NK) line. A goods line comes into the station with a connection to platform 4. The curve into the NK line from Limerick Check and connections into Careys Road sidings are seen.
Peter Barlow

Limerick Colbert Station Yard with the Limerick District steam and a vintage coach for the breakdown crew, 15th May 1982.

The breakdown train, in Colbert Station Yard, showing the ruggedness of the crane. On each side of the machine is a steam powered cylinder; the left-hand one is visible. Steam was created in a coal-fired boiler placed inside the metal shelter. Very low-geared drive to the jib; very powerful.

A Great Southern & Western Railway bogie coach, sitting in Limerick Colbert sidings on 15th May 1982, now used by the permanent-way department, as accommodation for their staff during a lengthy job.

Limerick Check cabin from the curve coming from Foynes Junction, August 1956.

Peter Barlow.

Tommy O'Brien, signalman at Limerick Check cabin, September 1974.

Limerick Check cabin, electric train staff machine and electric equipment to operate points at Foynes Junction, January 1974.

Facing page: Limerick Check cabin track diagram and a 20 ton freight train brake van, September 1974. The guard riding in the van could use the hand brake to help hold back a train running on a steep falling gradient.

Limerick derelict loco shed and site for a new maintenance garage for Bus Eireann beside the Foynes Junction line, September 1974.

A train for the Ennis – Athlone line, August 1956. The prominent junction signals apply to the track they stand beside.
Peter Barlow

Looking to Colbert Station from Check cabin, September 1974. Diesel hydraulic 401 class No. E428 either making a shunting movement or heading for points to enter the Up Main line.

No. 184 hauling an Athlone – Limerick Colbert rail tour, in May 1984, about to pass Limerick Check cabin.

No. 171 was on the same tour but was banned from using the Athlone – Limerick route.

No .184 has its fire taken out and the firebars cleared of 'clinker' ready for a fresh fire to be lit, May 1982.

No. 171 and No. 184 make a grand sight out of Limerick Colbert en route for Kilonan Junction, Nenagh and Ballybrophy.

Junction signals at Killonan. The double track from Limerick Colbert merges into single track outside the signal box, September 1974.

Killonan Junction Signal Box, September 1974.

Facing page: The electric staff instrument at Killonan Junction, September 1974. The equipment for the single line to Limerick Junction is in sunlight and the signalling instrument for the double track to Limerick Colbert is in shadow. The Booking Desk carries the Train Register in which the signalman records the time of every bell code received and sent, the title of the trains and which way they were going.

Signals for level crossings, near Lisnagary, on the branch line from Killonan to Ballybrophy, September 1974.

Lisnagary Station and level crossing with 041 hurrying back 'light' to Limerick. September 1974.

Dromkeen signal box, September 1974.

Knocklong Station with 052 hauling the Shelton Abbey ammonia train, hurrying down the grade towards Cork, December 1982.